T0401302

ANIMAL CHAMPIONS

ANIMAL CHAMPIONS OF THE JUNGLE

By Madeline Tyler

KidHaven
PUBLISHING

Published in 2023 by **KidHaven Publishing,**
an Imprint of Greenhaven Publishing, LLC
29 East 21st Street
New York, NY 10010

© 2021 Booklife Publishing
This edition is published by arrangement with
Booklife Publishing

Edited by: Emilie Dufresne
Designed by: Drue Rintoul

All rights reserved. No part of this book may be reproduced
in any form without permission in writing from the publisher,
except by a reviewer.

Find us on

Cataloging-in-Publication Data

Title: Animal champions of the jungle / Madeline Tyler.
Description: New York : KidHaven Publishing, 2023. |
Series: Animal champions | Includes glossary and index.
Identifiers: ISBN 9781534541450 (pbk.) | ISBN 9781534541474
(library bound) | ISBN 9781534541467 (6 pack) |
ISBN 9781534541481 (ebook)
Subjects: LCSH: Jungle animals--Juvenile literature. |
Jungle ecology--Juvenile literature.
Classification: LCC QL112.T945 2023 | DDC 591.734--dc23

Printed in the United States of America

CPSIA compliance information: Batch #CSKH23: For further information contact Greenhaven Publishing
LLC, New York, New York at 1-844-317-7404.

Please visit our website, www.greenhavenpublishing.com.
For a free color catalog of all our high-quality books, call toll free
1-844-317-7404 or fax 1-844-317-7405.

Photo Credits

All images are courtesy of Shutterstock.com. With thanks to Getty Images, Thinkstock Photo and iStockphoto. Throughout — Cocos.
Bounty. Front Cover&1 — apple2499, CWIS, Anan Kaewkhammul, Milan M, Elnur. 2–3 — Teo Tarras, PRANEE JIRAKITDACHAKUN. 4–5
— Cristi Popescu, Ondrej Prosicky. 6–7 — Frank McClintock, Damsea, nattanan726. 8–9 — Atthapol Saita, Glenn Young, Enrique Aguirre,
Travel Stock. 10–11 — jeep2499, Daniel_Ferryanto, Sanit Fuangnakhon. 12–13 — Jukka Jantunen, Shutterranger. 14–15 — mark higgins,
Misbachul Munir, LeonP. 16–17 — Jonah Goh, Andreas Gradin, nattanan726. 18–19 — LABETAA Andre, Patrick K. Campbell, SachinSubran.
20–21 — Jiri Hrebicek, Eric Isselee, Marc Lechanteur, Vladimir Wrangel. 22–23 — Lori Jaeski, Purino, Darren Baker, Denis Kuvaev.

CONTENTS

Words that look like this can be found in the glossary on page 24.

IN THE JUNGLE

Jungles are <u>tropical</u> forests. They are very hot and very wet. Some animals live at the tops of the trees, some animals live on the jungle floor, and some animals live somewhere in between!

Let's meet the **animal champions** that call the jungle their home!

WHAT MAKES AN ANIMAL CHAMPION?

Animal champions don't always have to be the biggest, fastest, or strongest animals around. They are champions because of the <u>adaptations</u> they have, or things they can do.

Come on! Let's head into the jungle...

THREE-TOED SLOTH

Sloths move so slowly that <u>algae</u> grows on them. This may not sound good, but it helps them <u>camouflage</u> against the green trees of the jungle.

Champion of Camouflage

Sloths are some of the slowest animals on Earth!

Sloths spend most of their lives up in the trees. Their long claws help them to hold onto branches.

Sloths can even sleep while holding onto trees. This is useful because they can spend up to 20 hours a day sleeping!

Champion of Long Naps

JAGUAR

You may think that most cats are afraid of water, but these big cats love swimming. Jaguars are very good swimmers, and they use this skill to hunt fish.

Champion of the Big Bite

Caiman

Jaguars have very strong teeth – they can bite through caimans and turtle shells!

Jaguars are also great at climbing trees. There are lots of trees in the jungle, so jaguars can climb up high to hide and to hunt.

Champion of Climbing High

Jaguars hunt during the day and at night.

ORANGUTAN

The orangutan is the largest arboreal <u>mammal</u>. Orangutans spend most of their time in trees, and their long, strong arms make it easy to swing from branch to branch.

Champion of Strong Swings

Arboreal animals are animals that live in trees.

Orangutans are very clever and are closely <u>related</u> to humans. They stay dry in the wet jungle by making nests within the trees and using leaves as umbrellas.

Champion of Staying Dry

Orangutan means "person of the forest" in the Malay language.

AFRICAN FOREST ELEPHANT

It can sometimes be hard to spot African forest elephants, so scientists <u>estimate</u> how many elephants there are by counting their poops!

African forest elephants are smaller than African savanna elephants, but they are very closely related.

The poop of African forest elephants is very important for helping the rain forest grow. Some trees grow better when an African forest elephant eats their seeds and then poops them out!

Champion of Poop!

CHIMPANZEE

Chimpanzees are very clever animals. They use sticks and branches to get insects from inside trees and logs. This means they can get to food that some other animals may not be able to find.

They also use stones, roots, and wood to crack nuts open.

Champion of Clever Eating

There are lots of deadly animals and plants in the jungle. To stay safe and not get hurt, chimpanzees use sticks to move and look at dead snakes and other things that could be dangerous.

Champion of Using Tools

A tool is a thing you use to help you do something.

MALAYAN TAPIR

Malayan tapirs have a very good sense of smell. They pee on jungle pathways so that other Malayan tapirs can sniff it and find their way to feeding and drinking areas.

Champion of Sniffing out Smells

Swimming is a great way to cool off in the hot jungle, and tapirs are very good at it! They also like to <u>wallow</u> in the mud, which might also be a way of getting rid of <u>ticks</u>.

Champion of Keeping Cool

Their snouts are good for smelling, but they also use them as a snorkel while swimming underwater.

GREEN ANACONDA

Green anacondas are very good hunters. They are mostly nocturnal, which means they sleep during the day but are awake and hunt at night. This means it is harder for them to be seen.

Champion of Hunting at Night

Green anacondas are the heaviest snakes in the world.

A green anaconda's eyes and nostrils are on the top of its head. This allows it to hide underwater and wait for <u>prey</u> to come by, before taking it by surprise and attacking!

Nostril

Eye

Champion of the Surprise Attack

OKAPI

Okapis have fur that is perfect for the jungle. It's very oily, so the water slides right off it, just like a raincoat. This keeps them dry on rainy days.

Champion of Not Getting Wet

Okapis have long tongues that are great for grabbing and holding food. An okapi uses its tongue to pull leaves off trees and put them into its mouth.

Champion of the Toughest Tongue

Let's see what animal adaptations we humans can use to be champions of the jungle!

Face paint and camouflaged clothes will help you hide like a sloth.

Shoes with good grip will help you climb like a jaguar.

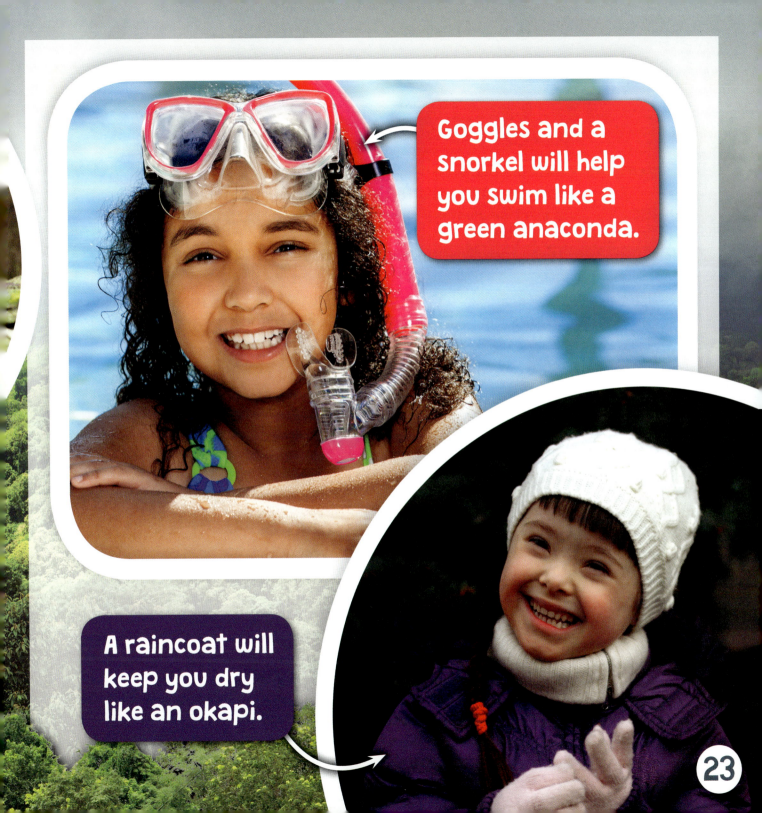

Goggles and a snorkel will help you swim like a green anaconda.

A raincoat will keep you dry like an okapi.

23

GLOSSARY

adaptations changes that have happened to an animal over time that help them to be better suited to their environment

algae a plant or plantlike living thing that has no roots, stems, leaves, or flowers

camouflage traits that allow an animal to hide itself in a habitat

estimate make a careful guess

mammal an animal that has warm blood, a backbone, and produces milk

prey animals that are hunted by other animals for food

related connected or part of the same family group

ticks small animals that attach themselves to people and other animals and suck their blood

tropical hot and humid

wallow roll in

INDEX